Peanuts

Contents

What Are Peanuts?	2
Where Do Peanuts Grow?	4
How Do Peanuts Grow?	6
Peanut Farms	8
Peanut Factories	12
Eating Peanuts	14
Index	16

Claire Llewellyn

What Are Peanuts?

Peanuts are the seeds of the peanut plant.

They are called peanuts because they grow in pods, like peas. But the pods are under the ground.

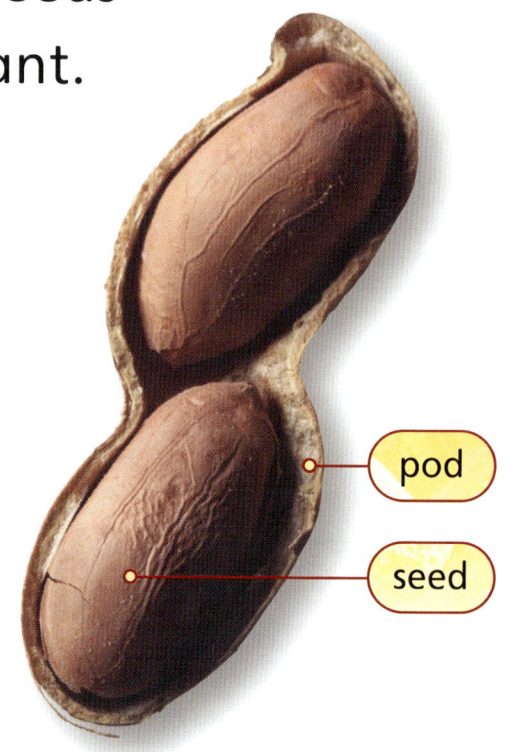

pod

seed

That is why peanuts are sometimes called groundnuts.

This peanut plant has been pulled up to show the pods.

Where Do Peanuts Grow?

Peanuts grow in warm parts of the world. Most of the world's peanuts are grown in these places:

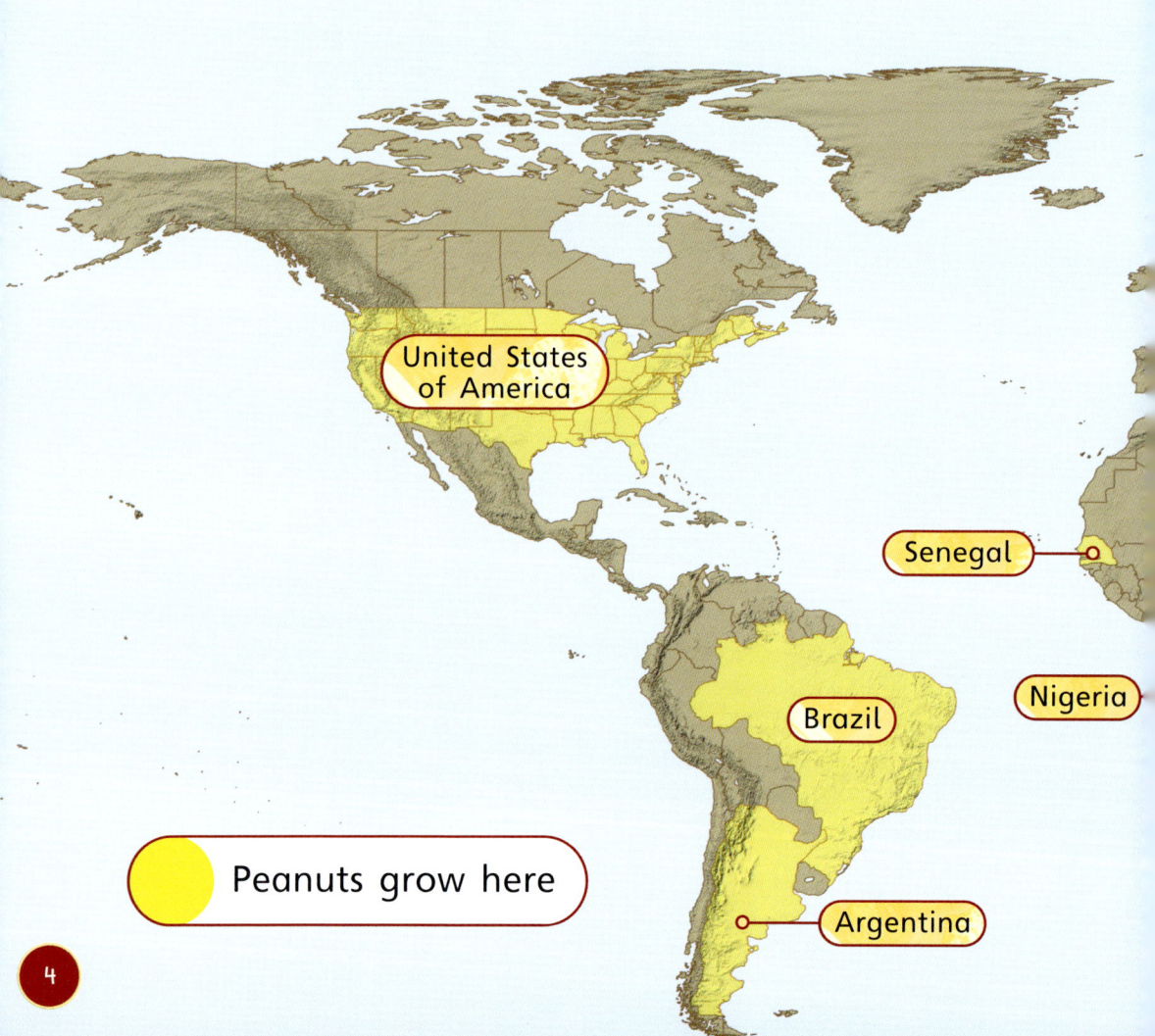

Selling peanuts in China

Selling peanuts in India

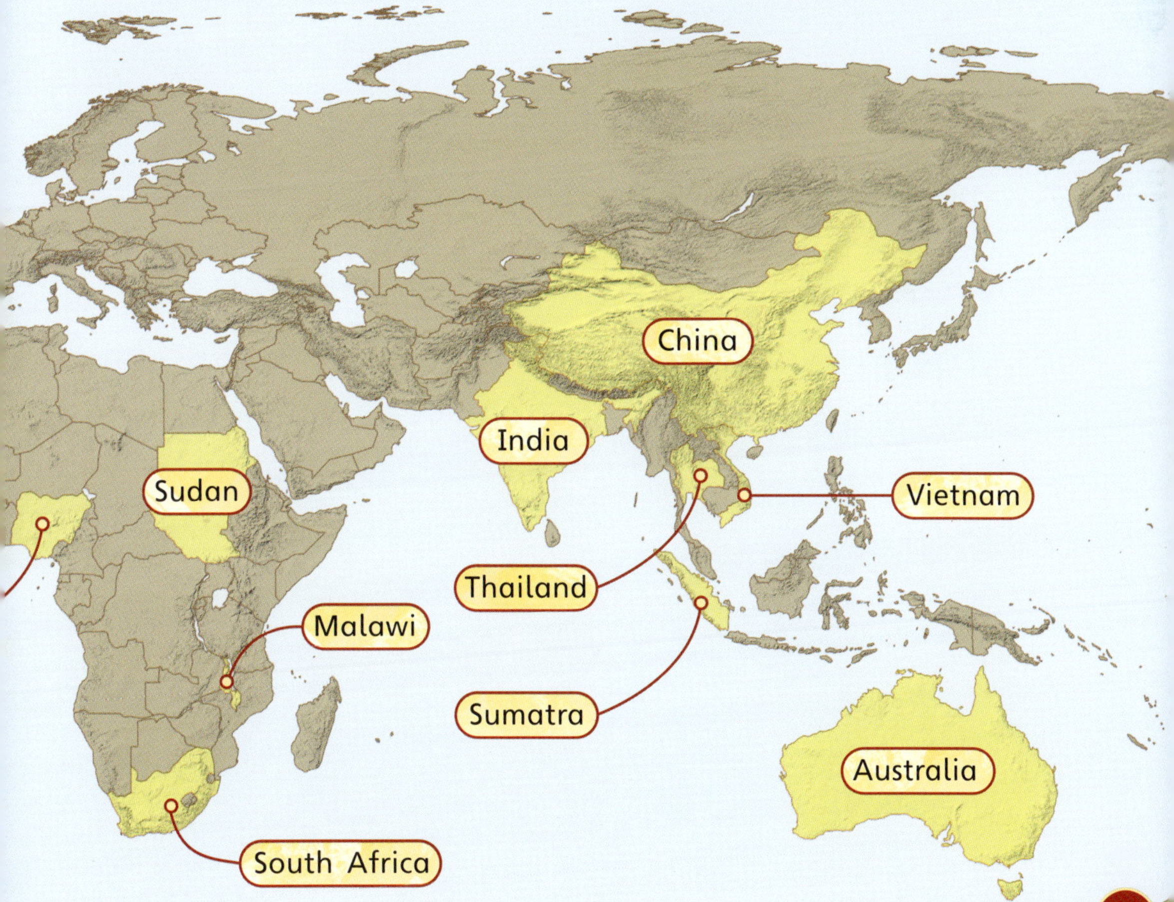

China
India
Vietnam
Sudan
Thailand
Malawi
Sumatra
Australia
South Africa

How Do Peanuts Grow?

Peanut plants grow yellow flowers on long stems.

The flowers on most plants grow towards the sun. But peanut flowers grow down towards the ground.

Then they grow into pods with seeds in them.

Peanut Farms

Peanut farmers sow the seeds in the soil.

The seeds are planted in rows, in large fields.

After four or five weeks, the plants begin to flower.

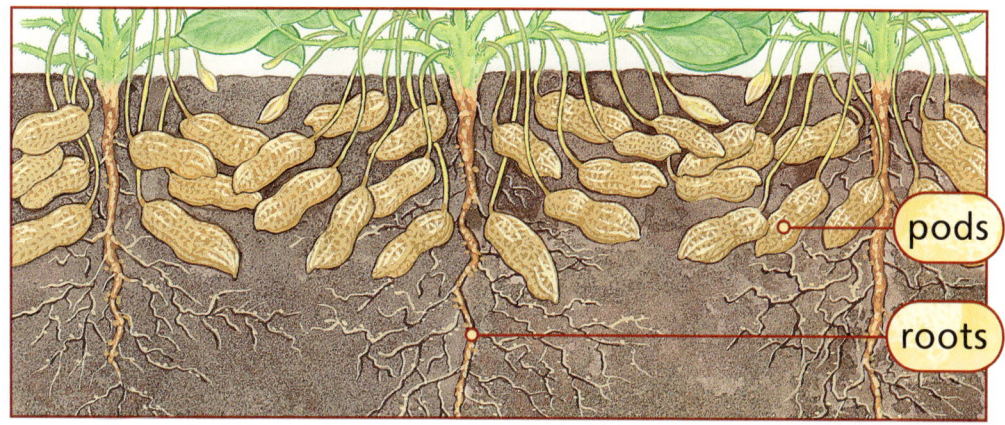

Then the petals drop off, the pegs go down into the soil and peanuts begin to grow under the ground.

Most farmers use tractors like this one to dig up the peanuts.

When the peanuts are ready, the farmer digs them up.

Peanuts drying in the sun

The peanuts are left to dry in the sun for a few days. Then they are packed into sacks.

Peanut Factories

The sacks of peanuts are sent to factories all over the world.

They are shelled.

They are cleaned.

They are roasted in an oven.

They are packed into bags.

They go to the shops.

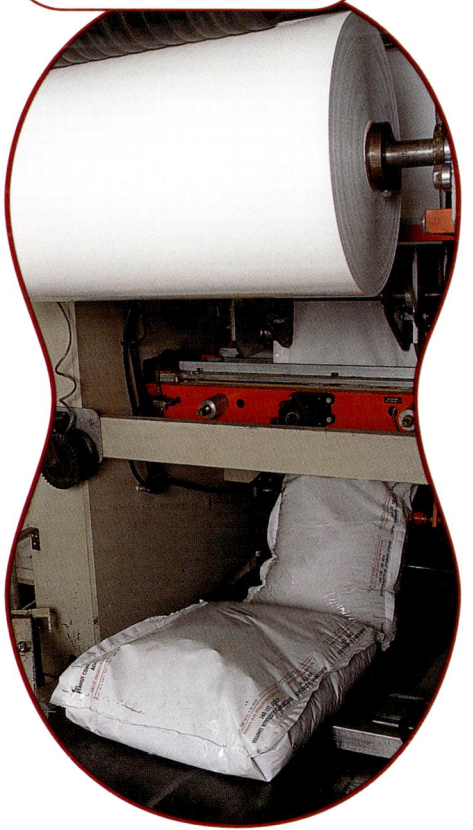

Eating Peanuts

Peanuts can be eaten in many different ways!

These children love eating **shelled peanuts**.

This **peanut butter** is tasty.

These vegetables taste good cooked in **peanut oil**.

This healthy **snack bar** is packed with peanuts.

This warm **peanut sauce** tastes great with noodles.

Warning:

Some people are allergic to peanuts. This means they can get very ill if they eat even a tiny piece of one.

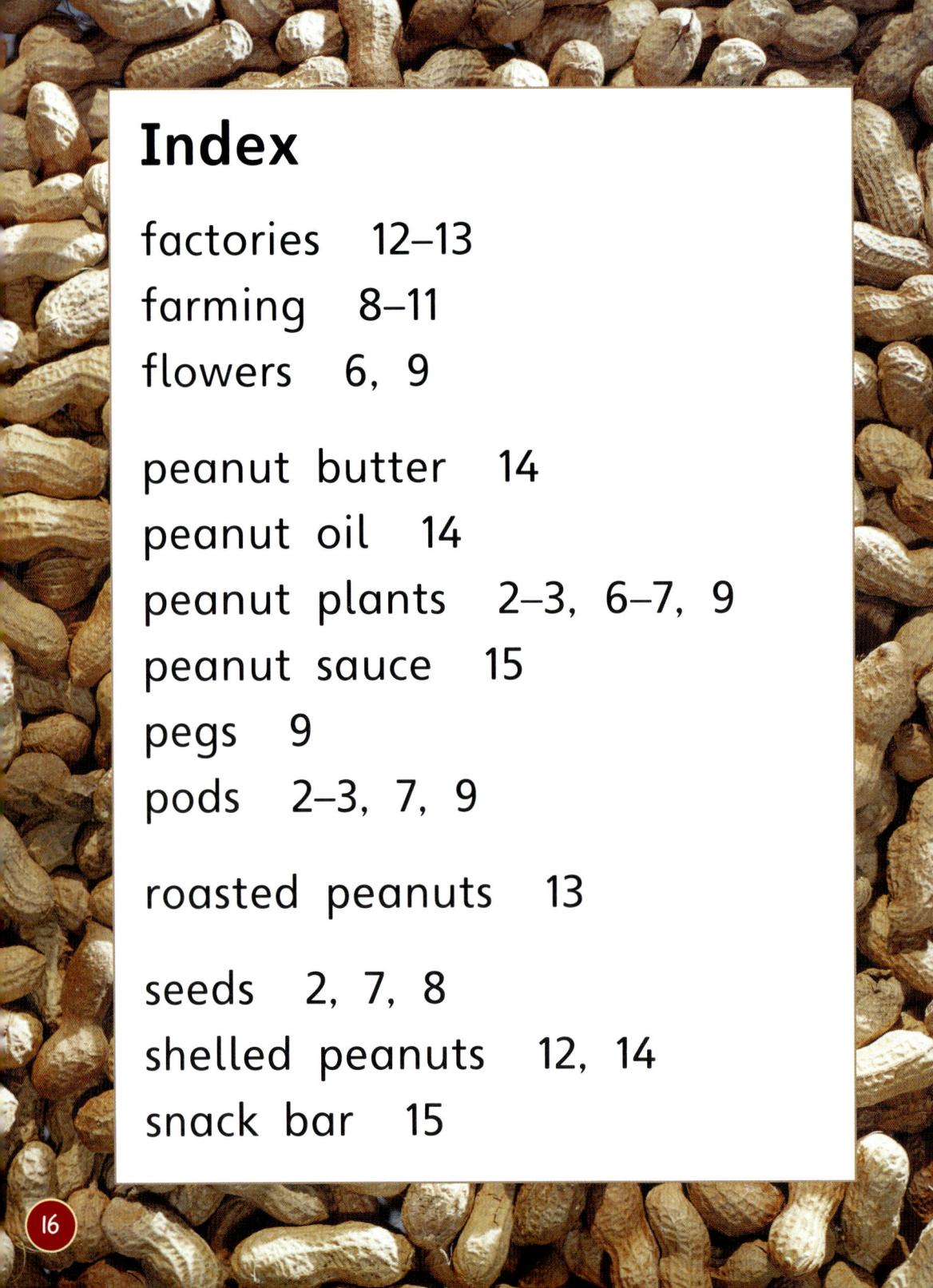

Index

factories   12–13
farming   8–11
flowers   6, 9

peanut butter   14
peanut oil   14
peanut plants   2–3, 6–7, 9
peanut sauce   15
pegs   9
pods   2–3, 7, 9

roasted peanuts   13

seeds   2, 7, 8
shelled peanuts   12, 14
snack bar   15